THE
Mysticism
OF
STONE

ISMANA CARNEY
& JOHN CARNEY

outskirts
press

Table of Contents

Introduction

"All Real Living is Meeting."
Martin Buber, *I and Thou*

I will never look at stones in the same way. It may happen to you, too. Read *The Mysticism of Stone* and your perception of our world's bones could be irrevocably altered. A good thing that, otherwise why engage in art? But it may come at a price. It did so for me. The reading of Ismana Carney's poems easily becomes a jubilant exploration of new realms of perception, feeling, and thought, an opportunity to experience the world of stone as a living kingdom of myth, story, vivid sensations and deep musings. I was at first quite buoyant in the space of this collection, but then I read the poem *Stone People* and to my astonishment, I wept:

I have stones who have been with me for most of this
ever-lengthening pilgrimage I call my life.
And each of them relocates with me, "crying out" abjectly
at any inkling of the notion of being left behind.

Suddenly, I remembered my rock. Many years ago, I found her (somehow, I knew the rock was a she) in one of California's canyons, way up on the rocky cliff next to a clump of dry moss. Sturdy and poised, resembling a small tower, she become my support in the shifting landscapes of graduate school, standing next to my computer as I typed away on the keyboard (I called her then "my writing block"). She slept on my pillow on the eve of all important occasions, her presence soothing and strengthening. Later, we traveled together from city to city.

Finally, we have arrived in coastal California, I began my work, and had an idea. Having been reading about the web of life and the interconnectedness of all phenomena, I decided to release my rock to the great ocean. I thought she would like to be free from merely human affairs, would appreciate becoming one with the vast, watery depths, bodies of whales brushing against her sides, seaweed coiling around her feet on the ocean's floor, that kind of thing. And so, I took my rock to a beautiful solitary beach along Highway 1, created a short ceremony of goodbye and bon voyage, and placed her on the sand close enough to the edges of incoming surf, which, I knew, would in time sweep her away. It did. The wave came and my rock was gone. Little did I know that I had just drowned my sister:

It's just how it is with stone people who were and are
kith and kin, anciently so and even now,
to discriminating humans.

Reading *Stone People* shook me. This poem transformed my rock from a vaguely animate, talismanic object into a vivid stone-person with feelings and experiences akin to mine. What I used to feel as a pang of periodic sadness (as in I wish I still had my rock) opened into a sense of deep loss. I was mourning my rock, and now I know I will mourn her forever. Now I know that she did not want to go. Now I know that she did cry. My own tears have told me so.

And not only that poem, but others in the collection, even the ebullient ones, evoke a sense of loss, if only fleetingly. And a touch of remorse, too. I began to wonder at this grief. Why was it there? Why in hiding? I reasoned that, above and beyond personal significance, the sudden onset of tears provoked by *The Mysticism of Stone*, attesting to the energetic vitality of the poet's writing, may also shed some light on the subject matter Carney chose for her collection and, like any poetry that is not afraid of depth, on the world we inhabit.

The last time I wept over a book was when I followed Prince Mishkin's descent into madness at the end of Dostoyevsky's novel *The Idiot*. I was sixteen at the time and in love with the doomed prince, who embodied, in his sacrificial innocence, one of the only stances of heroism available in the cultural imagination of communist Poland. There, the secret police killed priests. Small wonder then that I wept when the prince succumbed, less to his illness than to the corruption of the world around him. Now, so many years later, what about the "Stone People"? What are the cultural underpinnings of my grief this time? Once identified, they may hold a key to the hidden territories of our individual and collective psyche, and to the power of poetry to illuminate its depths; and since that which we repress controls us, it may behoove us to venture into these spaces for glimmers of self-illumination.

But maybe "key" is too genteel a word. Maybe what we are looking for is an axe, the one from Franz Kafka's injunction to writers whose writerly task is to deliver a blow to "the frozen sea within" each of us. The poem—the entire collection in fact—did deliver such a blow to my own frozenness that barred me once from a genuine relationship with my sister rock. It helped me recognize that I regarded the rock as a magical tool, thus appropriating her agency and making her an object of use. It did not occur to me then to talk to the rock, to ask her questions and to listen to her answers, which would have come, I know that now. I was like the protagonist in Wislawa Szymborska's poem *Conversations with a Stone* who thinks she wants to learn what it's like to be a stone, but who doesn't have the faintest idea of how to go about it:

I knock at the stone's front door.
"It's only me, let me come in.
/.../
"You shall not enter," says the stone.
"You lack the sense of taking part."

As much as it was my own, my frozenness was also a part and parcel of a larger, cultural frozenness that enables indifference to our biosphere and its denizens: plants, animals, indigenous people, the elements, and yes, the stones, our origin and our cradle. We, the progeny of the military-industrial West, we A.K.A, the Masters of the Universe, are deaf to Earth's cries because we do not think that the world is really alive beyond the movements of cells involved in bio-chemical transactions. Life: the mere pulsations of mechanical bios—that's about it for us. The rest—nature as in-spirited sentience—we think a fantasy. Even when, alarmed by ecological disasters, we begin to consider anew the fact of the all-around relationality of life itself, we rarely engage the non-human world as kin. We rarely if ever talk to rocks and trees. We almost never listen. All too often, human-to-nature kinship becomes an aspirational metaphor relegated for use in moments of holiday reverie, contrition, or activism.

But so much more is needed, a whole new, enlivened way of envisioning our relationship with the Earth must commence, for, as David Suzuki stated, "The way we see the world shapes the way we treat it." And if we see rocks as sentient, then we will at least try to treat them, and other beings like them, better. So, we need to start talking to rocks. And to other non-human beings like mountains and rivers. We need to start doing that now. And since we forgot how to do it, Ismana Carney's poems will teach us, enabling this vision of an enlivened world to emerge in us and around us. It may not be as difficult as all that, for it is already all around us, a longing welling up at the heart of stone to reach us humans benumbed by our forgetting of Earth's sentience. If we can learn again how to hear the stones cry, laugh and tell stories, then maybe we could also hear the whales and their death songs, the trees weeping, the animals cavorting and yelping; maybe then we can become attuned to the pain of the indigenous tribes who continue to suffer at our hands but whose life-centered cosmologies harbor knowledge that may save all of us in the days to come. And then everything may change.

Behavioral scientists tell us that compassion may be stronger in us than the instinct to survive. By recognizing the pain and joy of aliveness around us, we are likely to re-discover this compassion, which in turn can reveal that we are in fact lovers, not killers. We can discover that we passionately love and want to protect that which is perishing. Overwhelmed by this remembered love, we may be able to halt the destruction of the planet, inviting the world to become newly alive to us, truly and fully, in a space of felt reality, beyond the decorations of metaphor. Read *The Mysticism of Stone*, and you may discover that you are in love with a rock, and that you don't want to her to drown.

What would being in love with the world-as-fully-alive feel like? Ismana Carney's poems offer some definite clues. First and foremost, it would feel, unsurprisingly, like being in a passionate relationship. In her poem *Stone City* these lines sing:

I am, you see, enchanted by the essence of you.

And again:

I hear your salt song in the whispering wind.

In her poem *Stoned Love,* being in love with the living world would feel vivid, pervaded by the beloved's presence out of which evolves a galaxy of love's articulations:

In the burning heart of stone
lies the history of all the world's loves.

However, true to the vision of love as intimacy of connection with a unique being, *The Mysticism of Stone* offers us an anatomy of engagement that bears much revelatory specificity. The very materiality of stones creates in this collection, rapturously detailed landscapes. It turns out that a heart of stone can give and receive love with a richness of expression both specific and boundless, stones being the "intelligences" that refract "the light and love of Creation here on Earth," intelligences that do not waft in a disembodied metaverse but are embodied in the stoniness of the stone. Although fed by the prolific, archetypal pageantry of an "immense articulation of sheltering stones", the poems remain focused on specific encounters, all uniquely vivid in their psychological and sensory scope, as in *Legend*:

Do you see what I see?
This stone as being—in and of itself?
Emerging force-filled, ferocious, like a
Gilgamesh, an Achilles, an Arjuna, a Beowulf—
telling of ancient heraldic worlds.

The entire collection becomes, to quote Szymborska again, a "knocking at the stone's front door" while realizing that the stone has no door but is openness itself, an intimacy of encounter between mythic presences— "There is, submerged under every pulsing stone / a living god striving, magnificent in the making" —and then the perceiving subject willing to venture into the immensity of inner and outer universes potentiated and revealed by stone's grace in the poem *Honeycomb*:

Stone is a bridge being across which
embodied intelligences or mythic incarnations
striding gloriously into the here and now,
show themselves beautifully,
like love eternally recurring.
And story themselves into any willing body-being,
so that what once was, can finally be spoken—

The "eternally recurring" love that manifests in stones and people protects this poetic undertaking from the hubris of human projections. In *The Mysticism of Stone*, humans and stones inform each other, but the prevailing affect of that communication is a listening-centered transport rather than an act of interpretative imposition. Sensitivity to the mysterious transmission occurring under the auspices of the Unknown pervades the entire collection as in *The Approach*:

As I near, I feel welcomed by the Unseen—
something so lovely about this feeling—
to be embraced-in-Spirit by a
congregation of enraptured stone.

Finally, true to the title of the volume, housed within each stone lies a mystical, ineffable potency abiding there since the dawn of creation as in these lines from the poem *Silence*:

It all comes down to stone—
Down to the stone silence
before the First Word was spoken.

The fecundity of this silent presence fuels this writing, much like the presence of the "dark peace" and the "fierce consciousness" sustains stone in Robinsons Jeffers's poem "Rock and Hawk", from which Carney's collection derives its name. Silence prior to ecstasy. Mystery prior to awe. Love underlying it all, hidden and silent unless invited into an encounter, miraculous in its specificity – such are, among many others, offerings of these poems.

So, off we go into the silent unknown, full of unnamed potencies? Or do we? That's just it. At the heart of *The Mysticism of Stone* resides a paradox. Mystical raptures often imply flight from the world. In these poems, however, the more mystical we get, the stonier we become. The more we journey into the stone's cosmic past, the sooner we return to presence on our benighted planet. Immersing ourselves in these stone poems, we may become more acutely sensitive to the life around us. Should we see in each stone a glimmer of our own spirit and psyche, maybe then we will see to it that it survives—this life, our lives. If not, then we will go back to the beginning, arising anew as stones flowing out of the stars, finding ourselves in *Stone City* once more:

In the beginning, I too was stone.
I will be stone once again—and will join you,
forever, starstruck.

Aleksandra Wolska
Santa Cruz, California, 2022.

Camera, Image, Life

Visual storytelling is a high calling which takes a lifetime of patience, dedication and passion to understand. A good story told in film, in a book, a painting, or a single photograph has the power to change, heal, influence, entertain, educate, inspire, as well as to elicit emotion, and maybe guide the course of someone's life. A series of images can shape culture and define a nation's identity. In the 20th century, fine art photography and photojournalism began to educate us about the world beyond our comfort zone. You have only to open a popular news or fashion magazine to appreciate the power of a single image. For me it's almost always a single creative photograph that grabs my attention.

I count among my friends many creative artists, writers, photographers, filmmakers, painters, teachers who have influenced and guided me. At Cabrillo College I studied photography with Gene Antisdel and Photojournalism with Dean Quarnstrom. I studied film and photography at the San Francisco Art Institute where I learned how to make better photographs and how to tell film stories. I worked in Hollywood beside some of the most talented filmmakers in the world. My life's journey has brought truly inspirational people close to me whose influences greatly helped develop my own creative vision.

Throughout my life, wherever I travelled my camera came with me. In my own creative work, there are times when I will see something that will just stop me cold and I will have to take a photograph. Often when I look through my viewfinder the light changes momentarily and results in an image, I didn't see at first.

At the Art Institute John Collier used to talk about the invisible magic that exists within the subject you are about to capture in your photograph. And Will Giles, a local photographer and one of my teachers who studied with Minor White, would always say that absolute magic can happen when all your senses lock into that "moment". To me the creative process is like alchemy. With photography, it's a flash of inspiration that can then manifest into an image which can be shared. If that work is truly inspired, it can resonate with people and bring meaning to their lives. It might take them out of their own reality or stir their consciousness or bring them great joy.

Photography is an art form I have practiced most of my life and will continue to pursue.

John Carney, Photographer
Scotts Valley, California, 2023

In the Beginning

Was it some thirteen billion years ago or
just yesterday—that the great Emergence began?

When *Being* encompassed existence
then began to measure time?

When, in the beginning, Hydros (Water) and Thesis (Creation),
Chronos (Time) and Ananke (Desire) inaugurated
a cosmic romancing of the highest order—
emanating as molten fire, spinning a trillion threads of gold
all a-shimmer, all a-glitter, all strewn about till Chaos suddenly
found herself beautifully ordered—a galactic logic-model.

And in the pearlescent heart of one swirling galaxy,
in one momentous instance, Gaia—Earth mother
was conceived in a heliographic storm of loving
and flung, molten, whirling into dark space—
Solaris roaring his own imperative to exist as,
in that same radiant instant, he began to die into himself.

Aren't we born precisely to die?
Do we not arrive with our leave-taking already in mind?

There is no end to beginnings, all of which end in themselves.
Eternally recurrent is the dance we dance, the song we sing.

Then, conceived in an alchemy of fire and ice;
appearing in quiet kinetic perfection, Phanes—life itself,
emerged with the new light of the first dawning day.
Shining resplendent, searching for his one and only disordered love,
he understood from the infinite consequences of their union that
Earth would know herself first as being; she would understand
herself to be sentient, and know her own nature as sacred.

And all this, spun in a star-struck loving so
elegant and extravagant, so secret and spectacular,
that in a singularly reflexive moment— a double-helixed
power move—the sacred code for all life was generated.
Adenine adores Thymine and Guanine adores Cytosine
and so, they begin their alchemical dance: a choreographed
celestial hieroglyphic, storying all life as we know it
on this beautiful, breathtakingly blue planet.

And what of stones?

When, after our own star, anciently named
Phoebus-Apollo or Mithra, Ra, Suraya or Tàiyáng Shén,
began his own cosmic dance—his sacred Nataraj; and
as the solar windstorm cooled under his dancing feet,
zirconian crystals clouded the cosmos.

Within each shimmering astral cloud
solar systems formed in myriad, and just as an infant,
nine lunar cycles within a beloved mother's womb,
is finally born into the bright light of a new day,
so too, our own star-born world, four billion years in the making,
emerged into a symphony of starlight—a diamond sky.

As each human being is unique by nature,
so too each of the five thousand races of stone
bears their own unique crystalline structure,
each contributing to the shining bedrock from which
Earth continually forms and shapes her apparent-self,
while an oceanic fire flowing deep keeps her forever starstruck,
forever oriented toward her own sacred origin.

But in the beginning; dreaming herself into being,
she coalesced like a poem in the cosmic round,
spreading her planetary body on a cooling crystal bed,
now become a stone canvas upon which
Creator imbedded the first sacred code:
a calculus so immaculate, so intent upon life,
that each first molecule found the perfect other,
and that perfect pair in turn found another, on and on,
until beautiful potencies, ensouled, intelligent, finally
understood the inexorable force of this merging and
laughed out loud to the heavens when suddenly
they *saw* themselves for the first time!
And there is, submerged under every pulsing stone,
a living god striving—magnificent in the making.

Now Earth rose from her bed of crystallized stardust.
Now she began to paint and sculpt and dance the world.
She danced for the waters: saline and sweet.
She prayed for the winds and sang down
the sun's love to release her own molten heart
volcanically, as women in their own blood-ways do,
bleeding, conceiving, giving birth.

And so, intent to increase her bedrock bones—
to make verdant space for even more life,
she began to weave a living tapestry
out of her bounteously beautiful body,
storying her myriad-aspected self into this world
replete with living creatures, with stones
and mountains to steady her tread
and river-deep forests, impenetrable
enough to hold her every treasure,
and yes, to keep all her secrets safe.

Stones Speak

In the Beginning fire was our original form
and soaring was our first starred nature.
Ablaze, with no end in sight, we were indeed ethereals.

Then, we were called to bear the weight of your world.

If you could only see, hear, taste and feel,
in ways beyond yourselves, your own origin,
you would know that we, you and I, are the same.
That we too contain heart, soul, mind, and purpose.

We love and we fall in love.
We live in families, in communities and nations too.
And, like the music of the spheres, we too, sing celestial—
have you heard us sing our salt songs?

Once we stood as mountains newly born and invincible,
ranging against an all-embracing sky, until compelled
by divine imperative to sing ourselves into submission
to even greater gods wielding fire, ice, wind, and rain.

They were called, apparently, to temper
our growing primordial grandeur and
to bring us to our knees in the service of Creation;
to bring this new forbidding remnant of starlight—
Earth-in-her-Angel—our gifts of sweet waters,
silted soil, bright air and meadows rich enough
for all living things to emerge.

And so, like you, we became
something other than our original selves.

As bedrock and in every other form of epidermal geologies,
serving all softer, malleable, more fragile life forms,
we sanctify in every moment, as some human beings do,
this light-refracted, deeply sentient, deeply sacred world.

Stone People

Wisdom keepers: these great-hearted ones,
offer a humble rest-stop to spirit
and sentient beings of all kinds: whether wandering
or waiting, grappling—death defiant
or simply needing sweet respite until the final release,
when forgiveness falls like spring rain,
the final destination crystallizes clear as day,
and life's struggle is finally won.

I have stones who have been with me for most of this
ever-lengthening pilgrimage I call my life.
And each of them relocates with me, "crying out" abjectly
at any inkling of the notion of being left behind.
I submit that this igneous insistence on inclusion
is non-negotiable and justly so, since for them
there can be no extenuating circumstances.

It's just how it is with stone people who were,
and still are, kith and kin, anciently so and even now.

Yes, and there are still brave hearts that may be found,
constant and unafraid of the incumbent ridicule consequent
to openly loving stones in ways beyond human reckoning.
I admit it freely—it's a Cult of Stone and I, I can testify to
this concrete cold fact: no stone has at any time, impeded,
constrained, diminished, disenfranchised, abused or forced
this precious life of mine to a standstill.

No, on the contrary, there is always pebble,
stone, or mountain, prepared to stand guard
when I walk into danger; always willing
to impart wisdom in despairing moments;
always ready to befriend unconditionally and always,
always when I'm driven to a point-of-no-return,
there's a broad-backed stone for me to lean on, to lean in to—
rock solid.

Star Dust

Stars are born by the millions each Earth-day;
strewn across an immeasurable indigo sky,
appearing suddenly like a cascade of diamond light
falling, whirling amidst the flashing feet
of some great dancing god like Shiva Nataraja:
Creator, Sustainer, Destroyer—in any event, all beloved.

And each glitteringly extravagant sun-star,
unable to withstand alone the charge of
its own impossible glory, spins around itself
a solar storm of fire, giving birth to a family—
moons, planets, asteroids, comets—simply to share the joy,
to bear the weight of the Divine Imperative—life itself,
and to keep each other good company—stone to the core.

And what of our own resplendent star?
He is a Friend who sees everything.
A luminary in his own right and light of my own life,
Suraya is the radiance permeating everything.
Lord of light and shadow, he gifts us
with an illuminated life to do with as we wish:
to strive for health, joy, purpose and inspiration
or to dive into the shadow finding meaning
in the incandescent depths of an even darker expanse.

But here, in the rose-gold dawn of *this* day, I feel
this silent stone sentinel vibrating by my side
as he opens his great heart to your burnished touch,
Suraya, your arrayed warmth, your kept promise
and he sighs as only stone can …

As for me, you are the Friend of my heart,
you are my life source, my everything:
my own soul's starlight, my seeking heart,
my pilgrim-mind, my very reason for being.

Heart of Stone

Someone said you
had a heart of stone.

We were, apparently,
the most mismatched pair.
This was frequently said.

I, like water, flowing tidal,
rising up from the deeps,
swelling and ripening under
the moon's lustrous gaze,
tugging at your fraying shirt sleeve.

You, with your razored intellect,
like granite glimmering in the light of love,
standing your ground—always.

I said, "I will, in every way,
no matter time nor tide,
no matter form or appearance,
always find my heart's way to you."

And this, transcribed here so beautifully,
in the tender brush of salted wave
rippling along the curved solid shoulder—
a magma flow stopped in the instant
at the first cooling, fluid, mercurial touch
and, in spite of itself, making landfall
in the name of love.

Shrine

There are places meant for
sacred ceremony;
for libations to be made;
for prayers to be said;
for hymns to be sung
to your own particular divinity.

Do you see the way this sandstone interface
is configured? How wind and rain,
ice and the sun's penetrating laser-light,
have conspired to sculpt this
stepped tabernacle set in stone?

Can you feel the draw of this sacrificial slab,
imbued with numinous presence, magnetic
enough that you find yourself drawing close,
compelled to engage in a gift-giving
of unmeasured grace, only *this* golden place
and you, will ever know?

Belle

"I've been waiting!"
She smilingly whispered, peering out
from behind her stone shield.

Captivated, I am stopped in my tracks.
"How long?" I ask,
as if I had unexpectedly
found a long-lost sister.
"And waiting just for me?"
"For *any* such as you, who actually *sees* me!"
she replied, delighted.

Ah! You are Belle! And yes, I know,
clearly, we are born of the same star.
Belle, what a beauty you are!
And, of course, well-met under
this late afternoon light raining down
and our own beloved star Solaris
shaking out his fiery tresses, as he
withdraws to the West, carelessly scattering
gold all across this glittering ground.

And you and I Belle, you and I,
calcinated contemplatives both,
we open to the quiet heart of light leaving,
displaying our own truth—petal tender
as a morning kiss from dawn's dewy lips
until, at the end of it all, this lovely day
surrenders herself to waiting night.

And you and I, beloved Belle,
in this place, in this moment,
become stone sisters.

I don't pretend to know why you became stone
but sister, I know why I did …

Silverback

And there he was …
in the gloaming, an anthropoidal perfection:
transcendent yet grounded, resonant in feeling,
like a sunstruck chord of love vibrating
in perfect stillness, shining viridian and
illuminated by a tender, tender light,
blue as a sky-stained ice sheer, translucent,
like a Buddha on the verge of Nirvana.

Something spun me around, you see,
as the sleet fell harder in sparkling shards
reflecting the piercing gleam of a silvered sunset,
as the pale air, fell below freezing.

What was it compelled me to look back?
The weight of a particular silence sounding?
The will of a deeper intuitive self?
Orpheus—spirit-keeper of the backward glance?
An inner call from a long, lost love?

I did turn around in that darkening mountain glen,
and remembered *that* Dian, enchanted in the mist, who fell
headlong in-love with Digit, her noble Silverback.

It was as if, not me, but *she* turned back for a final glimpse!
And I, their go-between, destined never to forget
him gazing upon *her,* as if there could be no other …

Stones bank great loves in no uncertain terms,
and love so enshrined between two of a different kind,
will reveal its storied relevance across space and time.

Honeycomb

Culture-bearers, expansive souls,
like so many suns across bright eons,
emerge in endlessly living forms.

Stone is a *bridge being* across which
embodied intelligences striding gloriously
into the here and now, reveal themselves
beautifully, like love eternally recurring.

They story themselves into any willing body-being,
so that what once was, can finally be spoken of—
the reminiscing, the safeguarding of memories
too precious to misplace, and all of this,
for own my attentive heart and for all our sakes.

Here, on this gently misted rise, a great-stone,
in resounding silence stands, mantled in green-gold,
time worn and honeycombed, holding me spellbound.

My soul's imagination takes flight ...

I am transported to the deserts of ancient Egypt
where I stand in a shower of bronze light
thinking about black and gold, and gossamer wings,
and strands of sunlight diffused in raw amber—
sunbeams captured in honey.

It's about a deeper, distinctly human wisdom
grounded in a higher kind of love, and
honey-concocted metaphysical nutrients—
the gift of healing given to us in the beginning
by one of the tiniest life forms: the sacred honey bee.

Sacred? Why?

Ask that of the ancient Sun God, golden-sceptered Ra.
Ask how we, his human creation, from the start
broke faith with him and in the breaking, broke his great heart.
Ask him then, how he, despairing like other creator gods,
understood, that he was destined for this very moment.
And so, our bright Ra wept bitterly, and bitterly so
in a radiant tearful downrush of godly lamentation,
all original sacred investitured oaths, abrogated.
And now Creation itself became suspect to the God of Light.
Its very existence punctuated by a growing question mark.

But then, a tiny exquisite representative for life
took decisive shape in the vivid nuclei of each godly tear
as it dropped sparkling onto golden ground.
Each jewel teardrop, you see, now took on the form of a honey bee
who in turn, took on the black and the gold—life and death;
and taking to the wing, did indeed sing the great Sun God
down from the dire edge.

But things had now changed between Ra and his human creation.
Now humans could do as they willed, having proven
their ultimate irrelevance to the Master Plan in terms of Creation itself;
in terms of the Divine Imperative; and in terms of their own tolerable,
and always predictive, small endings.

And Ra sings ...
"All the worlds are mine own.
Dancing the seasons is the sacred work
and all who are mine, dance sacredly for me.
Mountains I raise, as do you your children—
teaching them to sing their own elevated truth.

All waters run to me in the depths of blue,
bearing the weight of all worlds.
Honeyed or in brine, in body or as ethereal,
waterways—all mine, dance sacred for me.

I have drawn the silver-ring of the world at dawn,
I have drawn the gold-ring of the world at day's end.
I watch the hours circle in and out creating
each fragile day anew: a day that welcomes me,
as does every newborn, reaching for the light.

Medicine Wheel

A lifeway, a pathway, a sacred walk …
A teaching, a discipline, a sacrifice …

Does anyone own this?
This land, this stone, this sign?

The First Peoples of this land
in fact, signed for it—contracted in stone
and *coded* in the ways of the Great Mystery.

Inherent rights …
Allodial rights …
Just by *being here first* rights …

Look, no need for further deciphering.

Those who "walk" it *know*
in ways too deep too fathom,
that it's simply a lost cause when it comes
to the pamphlets, the booklets, the guides, and the maps;
to the theories, the speculations, the assumptions, and
the unashamedly mis-representations, mis-interpretations.

Oh! And not to mention the impotent post-scripted apologies
on the part of our parks, the priests, and academia—

Always too little …
Always too late …

And, most of the time,
just plain wrong.

Star People

We fell from the stars …

We've been playing the fool …

Ever since …

Stone Sisters

They stood tall, stately, virginal,
like goddesses of war striking for peace even
while bound to stakes splintered deadly,
and with embroidered satin robes fluttering
in the gold-dusted desert wind of Kandahar.
Like exotic captive birds brought from afar,
they watched the encircling beasts;
status notwithstanding, every one of them base.

Jiê Jie, eyes gazing into and beyond the horizon,
dreamed of the evening seascapes she so loved.
Always yearning for silver-lined other possibilities,
she could mystify any and all, yes, even here,
shining in sordid silk tatters of teal blue chiffon.

Mei Mei, with eyes downcast, was beautifully self-effaced.
Her silvered sage-green gown torn, as brutal as torn could get,
and revealing too much to bear for any sensitized soul,
yet still, her inborn stature put to shame that deadly stake.

Xiaio Mei, the youngest, was standing her ground,
her strong foot pawing the aged planked wood,
hands wrenching that offending stake.
Her narrow wrists were bloodied by her resistance to rope.
Her exquisite body, nubile, only recently virginal,
disclosed her wound, as the harsh hot winds
lifted the blood-streaked, stained silk layering around
her young body, unprepared for the violence of the theft.

But here …
lost on the slave-trading grounds of Kandahar,
with a great beating heart like that
of her beloved dun stallion—love of her girlish life,
with droplets of blood the color of garnet fringing her hem,
Xiaio Mei rises above her tragedy, grasping each
ravening, bedazzled, lusting fiend in the close surround
with the eyes of a Medusa.

And yet and so, these three Graces,
Frayed and stung, torn and bloodied,
still shone white as alabaster translucent
and silvered under Dawn's new light.

They stood and gazed beyond all this.
They wondered at the misguidance;
They wondered at the misplaced love;
They wondered at misbegotten truth.
After all, their loving family; elders, parents,
aristocrats and scholars all, succumbing to
a simple twist of fate, had sold them for a pittance.

They gazed at each other, these three sisters,
heads held high, unbroken like wild horses,
knowing now the abiding shame
only corralled women know.

Unspoken but understood they knew now
there could be no question of disloyalty,
no thought of betrayal, no idea of more or less love,
it could only be all for one, one for all.

The bidding began ...

The men adamantine, their intent brutal.
Some powerful, some admittedly, quite beautiful;
Some wise, some in love-at-first-sight;
Some wealthy in the ways of the world;
Some wealthy in the ways of Spirit—
But all, all mad with desire and ready to sell
anything, everything to secure all three treasures,
each one more exquisite than the other.

The three sisters, wrist-bound each,
blood-let but standing strong, watched the horror
rising darkly in the round, and prayed for,
trusted in a saving grace to come
in any shape, in any form, at any price.

Under the wooden platform
upon which they were staked,
through a small crack in the loose planks,
Xiaio Mei caught a slight movement.

While *Mei Mei* heard a quiet voice,
strong, gentle, deeply compelling.
"Are you willing to come with me?
I cannot promise you much, only
safety and peace, and freedom
of a kind."

Then *Jiê Jie* felt him nearby.
Even unseen, she understood
his own desire, his strength, his fortitude.
She knew, if the three were willing,
he would not leave, unless it was with them all,
and her wise heart quivered.

She softly spoke. "Who are you?"
He said, "Lady, it should not matter now
but know that I am like no other."
To *Mei Mei* who whispered,
"How are you able to do this thing?"
He shyly replied,
"I am able to wield my own will, beautiful one."
Then *Xiaio Mei* stamped her foot,
"Rescuer! Show yourself!"
"I will," he assured. "But only when I have
made good our flight to freedom!"

The three sisters, with knowing glances,
nodded their assent as the bidding all around
reached a frenzied pitch and the fevered desert
rose up in a horde of dust-devils spinning, blinding.

Then, in the quick of an eye, they were transported
into a new world, golden, vast, empty, drawn with a
porcelain sky fused to the pearled horizon and with

Heaven descending in a rhapsody of blue.
Now they ran, fleet and free across the land,
glorying in the light and the deepening shadows.
They ran and ran, almost flew, across stone-tumbled expanses,
flinging fragments of shattered dreams and virginal hopes
into the arms of a deeply compassionate sky.
They ran until there was nowhere else to run.
They ran until they were sated, were finally ready
to be exactly where they were—together as one.

And there …
seated inside a small circle of red stones
was a very small man bred from a special race—
he was stone.

The three sisters approached and quietly sat
in front of him—as in a half-moon,
and they gazed upon him
as twilight reached down covering them
with a shimmering veil, fragrant with sweet relief.

Then he gently spoke:
"Will you three jewels stay by my side?
I cannot promise you much, only safety
and peace and freedom—*of a kind*."

"I can." *Jiê Jie* spoke as the stars
brightened in the darkening sky.
"*I will*." Mei Mei whispered as she gathered
a small crystalline stone to her moonlit breast.
"Yes!" *Xiaio Mei* said as she pawed the
golden ground with her small proud foot,
as her beloved dun stallion would have done.

Deer Fish Shaman

The approach needed to be attentive, almost reverent.
I was indelicate enough, stumbling among a basalt fall
trying to make the rough ascent before day's end,
when unexpectedly, on a tapering verge
too narrow for comfort at cliff's edge,
he introduced himself on a rough stone wall.

A pilgrim at heart; playing on holy ground
in a petroglyphic preserve, I gazed deeply
upon this entrancing figure and shyly asked
if I could name him, for my sake, if not for his.

"I will name you Deer Fish Shaman
because you move effortlessly between worlds—
Earth and Heaven, here and now, in order to
sustain, inspire and protect your people.
Deer has gifted you with the symbol of his being.
Look! his antlers on your willing brow reach for the sky
while drawing down your own spiritual ascendancy,
the nature of which is *his* own nature.

Deer Fish Shaman—
You shine the light of the forest whose splendid diffusion
is translated in your world as freedom of spirit.
And in the wisdom tradition that speaks of the innocence
of wild things who give their own lives that we may live,
and in so doing must be honored in song and dance,
in prayer and ceremony, I hear your teaching.

And then, my new teacher, you took two relatives:
silver fish and dancing deer, brightly flashing, mercurial,
and with magic enough to feed, as rivers feed the ocean,
your evolving soul.

Imbued now with the spirit of two sacred beings,
I see your soul's deepest orientation: your east-west meridian
pulsing with ever-present hidden imperatives—
and all are enchantments."

The Kiss

"I'm yours," you said.
And gathered me up in your arms
like there was no tomorrow.

"Don't talk about Heaven or Earth—
They have no say in this …
I'll never let you go," you said.

You were here to stay …
it seemed.

I gave you all of my heart
as I reached for you lips.

"And this kiss,"
you whispered, "will last forever."

Sentinel

Just as ferocious stone *Komainu* guard
the ancient Shinto shrines of Japan;
just as the noble Sphinx sentinels Pharaoh's tomb;
and Griffin and Winged Lion are stationed
at the time-worn gates of ancient Persepolis, so too,
this solitary stone stands watch over this ancient land.

On an overlook, under an emblematic sky,
sheathed in stone the color of polished bronze,
he extends his vigilant gaze across this
infinitely vast and boulder-strewn expanse.
Only the silver-rimmed horizon ornamenting
Earth's shimmering hem arrests his view,
reminding him of his decreed place at *this* lonely Gate.

Who and what is he guarding?

Some places in this sacramental world
need to be protected: need to remain
immaculate, pristine, primal, intact.
Some enshrine secrets meant to be kept.
Some in themselves are Earth's own stone temples
inviting her devotees to bring sacred offerings,
their dances and songs, and soul commitments.

Be assured: this stone-cold sentinel, vigilant
by nature, an isolate, faithful and grim,
will challenge all desecrators who
stumble upon *this* unsigned holy ground
defacing, defecating, despoiling—
knowingly or unknowingly intruding upon
and plundering its structural sanctity

And our sentinel's stern, headlined response?
"Unstable woman breaks ankle leaping from rock to rock."
"Man found unconscious—suffering heat stroke."
"Disobedient child bitten by young rattlesnake."
"Off trail hiker disappeared—still to be found."

Vertical Smile

Friend!

Who on earth are you sending this
upside-down smile to?

Some great Holy Fool?
A Divine Jester?

Hey! I'm always up for
a good cosmic laugh!

You know—
the kind that generates a flood of tears?

Oh! Did I just miss the joke?

Hey! It couldn't have been *that* funny!

I see the little guy behind you!
He slept right through it!

Darn!

The Approach

Approaching this rock-strewn abode,
I wonder if I am worthy. Today is supernatural
and as rare as, "and the clouds parted!" or like Moses
in the desert scrub, coming suddenly upon a "burning bush".

Here, I'm welcomed by a *punctate little bear*—
an exquisite emerald-gold scarab, signifying
in ancient terms, life as everlasting, of days always new,
of second chances and other divine mercies.

As I near, I feel welcomed by the Unseen—
something so lovely about this feeling—
to be embraced-in-Spirit by a
congregation of enraptured stone.

It is now dusk when the light intensifies
and reverent shadows draw close as remnants of
scattered golden light burnish these stone people.

I draw close to the vibrating heart of these new friends,
entering an ancient talus of encircling stone.
Then in an atmosphere hushed and scented
with the dusky fragrance of a burning desert,
caressed by cooling evening breezes,
my arms raise, palms skyward.

Drawn deeper into this statured precinct of stone,
I defer to their siliceous world, paying homage to them
and, in turn, am hailed and well-met by each
in the ways of the Great Mystery.

You might say that I *feel* my way into intangibles;
unhesitatingly say "Yes!" when invited into
the transcendent unknown and, at this very moment,
have no doubts in joining this beautiful convergence of stones
who have me riveted to *this* holy space, to *this* holy light!

Stone Angel

Stone Angel, this song is for you!
I saw you on the way to D.H. Lawrence's Kiowa Ranch
in Arroyo Seco—Dry Creek, New Mexico.
I was on a pilgrimage, you see: a sacred journey
to hallowed ground—in the literary sense of things.

Then, when I saw *you* watching me drive by and
when I *heard* your angelic sigh mingled with
this enchanted land's fragrant gold-shot blue air,
and then, with your almost imperceptible feathered kiss
on my cheek, I felt that you had blessed the intention.

Why was I taking this journey?
I wanted to visit the Englishman's shrine.
I wanted to get a sense of the spirit of this place
where he had lived and loved, and returned to
again, and again to write amongst his Muses three:
Lady Brett, Mabel Luhan and Frieda von Richthofen
who abandoned her children for love of the man.

I wanted to stand at his tomb and tell this inspired iconoclast:
a coal miner's son, at core rough as torn coal-dusted burlap,
that I too—an Essex girl, felt that I had touched Heaven's
fringed and beaded hem, when I first gazed upon a
Kachina cloud-dancer tripping the light fantastic across
a dazzling turquoise, coral and silver New Mexico sky
and understood in the deepest ways that *here* the notion
of a biblical Garden of Eden becomes irrelevant.

And like you, Mr. Lawrence, I am also called again
and again, to return for that infusion of sanctified air
in the blue heart-vein, in the crimson arterial flow,
in the body and the bone polished gold on the brightest of days;
and of silver moonlight on snow-driven indigo nights;
and knowing deep in the soul that the spirit of *this* place
belongs first to the *first* people on this land.
Because, like you Mr. Lawrence, I am after all,
only a privileged guest in someone else's true home.

Scorpio

He said he was a Scorpio, I said I was a Capricorn
with Sun in my Ninth house and that I had
a *thing* going with that gold-showering star.

In South Africa he was a dealer in diamonds
but much more poetic and meaningful to me:
he called *Baba Ya Simba*—George Adamson—friend!
And, like George, he too learned to live with lions in the Serengeti
and had become as fiercely protective of all wild things.

My Scorpio was tawny blond with eyes sea-green and deep,
heart tremblingly so and leonine, in look and feel,
positively electromagnetic. Did I say "*My* Scorpio?"
no, that was not true but it took some thought
as I watched his eyes watching mine, sailing from St. Helier
on the Channel Island of Jersey to St. Malo in Brittany
for an early sunset supper and a summer swim in the English Channel.
I remember it was a warm summer evening under the silver light
of a full moon, our bodies fluidly entwined.

But I was too young, still finding my feet, constantly curling
my toes on the hardening ground of my own becoming.
Scorpio wanted a new bright star in his own personal firmament—
lions in the Serengeti and all. He wanted to mine and cut and polish:
to set and encircle me in a band of gold; to display me like a crown jewel.

I do admit it … there was a moment when I thought
I could gaze into his eyes and find myself there—always.
And then, I thought of the lioness that *Baba Ya Simba* loved
precisely *because* she was wild-born and free to live
as she was meant to, knowing herself to be
exactly who she was, nothing more, nothing less.

And so, as we sailed back to St. Helier in silent reverie,
gazing knowingly into each other eyes, sensing our own true place
as I began to see my way to even farther shores—life unencumbered—
and me in the rough, free to say, "Yes!" at each personal turn
in the ever-unfolding story that was only mine to tell.

Jade Master

I had my sights set on high-walking the Pinnacles trail.
Everywhere immense rockfalls of colossal yellow boulders
punctuating the woodland floor greening in the shade,
while rising to the sky, an immense grey-stone escarpment
shot horizontal with curvatures of light delineating the crush of time.

Suddenly, coming around a bend, your quiet smiling presence
grounded my gaze, drawing it into the canyon depths and
there you were! Marked deeply, dignified by age-in-time.

Recognition instantly took hold as I gazed into your beloved timebound
face; the deep-set meditating eyes; the craggy boned, roughhewn features,
and your ever-quiet smile brought it all back to square one.

There at the edge of the trail, I wanted to climb down to greet you,
palms together—body proximate.
"Jade Master, I *see* you and I am here!"
"Stay above my beloved!" you commanded.
Then even more gently, "Stay where you are my child."

Revered teacher you are here! And
you have become *Gongshi*! Stone Spirit!

Remember wise one, those ancient shining sacred stones
that, like the full moon, encircled our meditations, our prayers.
"They are intelligences," you taught, "refracting the
light and love of Creation here on Earth. Learn now to love them."

You guided us to aspire to *their* attainments saying,
"The stone will teach you, just listen, look and learn."
Then you smiled, like a sunrise on a new day.

And now here you are Jade Master in another world,
in another time and I have found you!

Gazing once more upon your principled being—the *zhòu* of you;
I see in your beloved face, creased and folding in upon itself,
there is joy and well-being—the *shòu* of you.

My heart moves through the time-worn fissures and crevices
that travel like conduits—hidden trails across your stone face
leading to the soul of all things—the *lòu* of you and I lovingly note
the tiny scored perforations in your blue and rust-grained face
that invite the day's shimmering light to glance through, and
the green evening mists to flow within and without; the breath
of life itself, to breath into you—the *tòu* of you.

Jade Master, do you remember when you spoke these words?
"In all of this, my sons and daughters, you will discover Paradise
within every being."

Then you mapped out the geography of Paradise within ourselves.
You invited us to set our hearts on discovering our own Jade selves—
our *Yù* nature: beautiful, refined, filled with grace,
conceived by Mountain and Water, in love.

You played your *Yuxiao*—your Jade Flute while we meditated
and learned that in *Yù* we could travel between Heaven and Earth,
and dream and teach of exquisite transcendencies as if
we were discussing shopping lists at the village market!

In Yù we become transparent like the sea—
knowing by the very nature of Jade, that we cannot but be
fragile and flawed, no matter the polished brilliance,
no matter the modest pose, no matter the courage of wisdom,
no matter the humility or compassion attained.

And so, venerable one, here we are now, together again
only now in *this* space and *this* time.

Jade Master, we have found each other as promised, and
as promised, I renew my abiding respect and undying loyalty.

Across eons, I have kept you close, holding treasured in memory,
our lifetimes together. And all your words, all your works,
and even deeper transmissions have eternally marked my soul.

Jade Master, my love, as you well know,
is unbounded.

Spiral

This whirling circle is a sacred thing in any realm of existence.
Ask any astronomer, geneticist, embryologist, mineralogist;
ask Zarathustra, Lao Tzu, Buddha, Jesus of Nazareth;
ask Prophet Muhammad, and Mirabai, St. Teresa or Rabia;
ask Ofra Haza, Eileen Jewell, Hildegard von Bingen or
Sting, Cat Stevens, Bach or Beethoven.

And then, on any land still deemed sacred, ask any
indigenous Traditionalist about walking on Earth
keeping the Sacred-in-Mind.

And here is this small spiral embedded and in love,
as I am, with stone and more than that, basalt—stone
closest to green Earth in her fiery volcanic labors
as, in microcosmic silences, she endlessly delivers
her own body-being into macrocosmic splendor.

Along with everything else it does, this small spiraling
spirit marked in stone is storying my own endless
pilgrimage between Heaven and Earth, Earth and Heaven
and in the process interlacing and interweaving
this tapestried life of mine without for a moment neglecting
the consequent debris—the concrete cold facts.

Spiraling galactic, inexplicably and hauntingly
beautiful, this small whirling mineral force of Creation
is dancing the power of life all by itself,
spinning out a fire-wheel into the universe
appearing then disappearing in an instant
like the brightest blaze of last light Sun leaves us
as a great-hearted gesture of filial love—
a promise of return, he has never yet broken.

And so, this stone-bound swirl of soaring lines
sings in minor the story of Creation's unfolding—
Spirit translated into finite terms—
an unbounded grace, a measureless love,
a spiritual calculus for the seeking soul.

Serpent

Exquisite relative mine, how you have been
maligned by some of my kind!

You were chosen by them to *host* in sinister image,
the Dark Archangel—Lucifer, a singular contradiction—
for he is also an emissary of the Light of Perfect Knowledge.

Forgive me, for in your graceful and quiet elegance
you have had to bear the symbolic weight
of human evil personified in the Western World by
the likes of Satan, the Devil, Iblis, Loki ...

Why you? Of all exquisite innocents?

And the result? Scapegoating, animal cruelty
and indiscriminate slaughter by some of my kind
even more frightening than the madness and mayhem,
orchestrated brilliantly like Creation itself,
by that illumined and darkly radiant, Archangel!

Look, there are many on this ever-spinning Earth,
thanks to the Greater Goodness, who have no idea
about this particular story—I mean the one about the Garden,
the Apple, the Free-thinking Woman, the Susceptible Man,
the Wise Serpent, and a particularly unreasonable God.

But there are other ones, beautiful serpent-relative mine,
never fear, these other ones, revere you, as they revere all beings.
Indeed, they believe you were sent to us from Creator's own sacred abode.

And you, a gift of highest signifying merit, you came to teach us
about sacred things, about a higher wisdom; about
eternal recurrence and transformation, and about
ethereal and corporeal realities—a kind of seeing that gives way to
visions and grace; to a deeper knowing of rivers and mountains;
deer and fishes, birds and stars, grass and trees and perhaps,
most important of all, prayer and stone.

Four Directions

This evocative image struck on New Mexico basalt,
has transported me to a dusky, grey-eyed dawn rising over England
with me twenty years in, in 1970 and innocent as a mourning dove.

Not knowing where to start my world pilgrimage,
I followed a white cloud whose perfect index finger
neatly split the newly sun-kissed sky and pointed,
in no uncertain terms, East.

And there, alongside the A20 with insistent thumb outstretched,
I put all my trust in that silver-lined, sky-shining, designating specter.

Long black hair, loose like Joanie Baez; hip-hugging
brown corduroy Levi's; V-necked turquoise t-shirt
revealing the curve; blue denim jacket; antique silver earrings;
and an ankle-length, monk-brown, hooded wool cloak
to announce and protect my holy intent.

My backpack was small and lightweight packed with
my own life's sacred texts: Nietzsche's, *Thus Spake Zarathrustra*;
Paramahansa Yogananda's, *Autobiography of a Yogi;*
Mirabai's *Songs of Devotion;* my British Passport;
an Arctic-proof sleeping bag in burnt orange
and one full change of clothing.

Paris first—six weeks in Montmartre, in a tiny attic overlooking
the Basilique du Sacré Cœur—the Nazarene's Sacred Heart,
architectured in a joyous celebration of stone that welcomed
my universal prayer each morning.
I could not fathom that there would be any other to match until
I prayed at the Blue Mosque—al Masjid Al'azraq in Istanbul;
then placed garlands of jasmine and orange blossom in the Taj Mahal;
meditated in the great Buddhist prayer caves of Ajanta,
and circumambulated Borobudur, the great Buddhist Stupa in Java.

From Paris to Italy, gazing at yet another cloud-arrow piercing an expectant
Florentine sky while admiring Brunelleschi's dome crowning the
Santa Maria del Fiore, the meaning was nothing but clear as crystal.
My sky signs took me not to Spain, not to Andalusia nor to the Alhambra
but again, East to the islands of Greece afloat on Homer's wine-dark Aegean.

And later … Eastward again to Turkey and Iran, India, and
the island of Java—not knowing then that there
on that magical island I would discover my original self,
she who is eternal, evergreen … and there it was
that my life-lens finally came into focus, where I began to
understand about being *here, now* and to know the *why* of me
—this time-round.

You are indeed a most powerful sign old friend of my heart!
Here in this volcanic petroglyphic disarray, I see you again,
only this time, not as a sky sign but as crystal-clear instruction in stone.

Where to now?

Bodhisattva

Beloved, were you not afraid when you made
your sacred vow? Did you not consider the consequences?
With your wisdom, your generosity of heart,
your even-keeled quietude, you said you were willing
to return to this world in any life form—*any* life form!

In the Sangha, I knew you loved Prince Siddhartha more.
While he, trying not to jeopardize you to envious eyes,
rose to austere distances, gazing into other worlds when you
drew near, in earnest circumambulation, sedimenting your own
Buddhist vows around the sacred altar in the stupa.

Beloved, yours was a moving meditation of such transcendence
we all were mesmerized, humbled in spirit or was it shamed?

Meditating with you in the chanting circle, seeing you,
feeling you rise in the light, I felt fear—my own lotus-body
becoming stone-bound—I dreaded losing the forbidden love
we had promised to consummate, in purity of body and spirit.

How could you so easily forget, my love?
Enlightenment was *our* shared goal.

We were born and grew into our days and lives together,
searching for, fighting for, sacrificing everything
for a shared destiny and so, we followed
great-spirited Shakyamuni to the very end.

Beloved, how did you reach the jeweled
hem of Nirvana without me?

And, how did you find it in your heart to—
I mean, when did your compliant heart fall so deeply
in love with this deceitful world?
And why did I not notice?
Where was I when it happened?
When did I begin to be left behind?

I remember that long-ago afternoon, with the sun's
burning rays filtering through the shade of wide-spreading
Banyan trees and the Bodhi tree under which our beloved
world-renouncing Shakyamuni became enlightened,
realizing himself, finally, as Buddha.

It was on a shining young day that the Buddha
called upon us to follow him on his sacred path.
And on that same auspicious day with shy, boyish hands entwined,
we vowed to strive for Nirvana together, side by side.

Then came that fateful moment when Lord Buddha
brought you into the heart of the Sangha's holy circle and
invoking Prajnaparamita—the Great Wisdom—
before us all, he *recognized* you! You were ready, he said.
You had indeed attained enlightenment! Nirvana was yours
and the gates of the Pure Land had opened for you.

My love, did you sense in that moment, as your eyes met mine,
that I was beside myself? How my heart shuddered and split,
my mind wheeling like a dying star vanishing into
a universe emptied of all meaning?

Then, just like the noble Bodhi tree, you rose and stood tall,
a paragon shining with bowed head before Shakyamuni
as quietly you spoke with the power of *vajra*—
irresistible as a thunderbolt, indestructible like diamonds.

You said you would put Paradise aside to embrace
the inexorable cycle of life and death—*Samsara*.
You would remain and then return, again and again,
until all despairing souls safely found their way
out of this impossibly paradoxical world.

Beloved, you turned Bodhisattva without me ...

I wanted to strike you then! You had promised to live and love
and die with me. We were supposed to continue as one
into our own enlightened, luminous forever ...

What made you look at suffering souls or invite wandering ghosts
to stay or want to comfort hearts destined by karmic weight to be broken?

Distraught, in that calamitous moment, I was heart-struck by
Lord Indra's lightning bolt. Blood turned to poison. Blood stained my lips.
Black blood ran arterial and white marrow turned to red in the bone.

As the Sangha, the sacred community, acquiesced to Lord
Buddha's sacred pronouncement, my silent curse
overrode their genuflections:
"If we cannot be as we promised my love—as one,
I call upon Lord Vishnu to bring you back to yourself,
as he himself once did to rescue his own soul,
only this time, as stone."

Don't ask what I promised in return.

And so, beloved, friend-of-my-own-heart, my own soul,
never fear, *I* will keep our promise to live as one,
and in all *our* lives to come!

You promised to return in any form!

I asked Lord Vishnu for like favors and here and now,
in this austere strange land, in this enchanted canyon,
my embodied stone heart will remain fused with yours
for as long as Creation itself is founded in stone.

Dwelling

Ancient ones—where on earth did you go?

Were you cut and crushed to the bone by those lesser ones
who dreamed your dreams—and then took everything?
They must have seen your treasured land, dusted-gold
and cooled green by subterranean springs that birthed
your sacred Water Songs. Songs sounding in the blue wind
and spirit-seeding the vegetal vitalities running viridian
in beautifully measured rows—food for life—just like
blood running blue in the vein rushes for the heart.

And then, deep-rooted and watered, sprouted and sweet,
life-giving green ones rose toward the light,
breaking into the sun-drenched day, reaching for the blue
in the depths of a receptive sky and giving themselves,
silently sighing, to your stone blade: the rip, the root, the stem,
and their exquisite blossoming selves—yes, there was everything to give.

Who was it then that ransacked and pillaged your other
young beauties—your daughters: life-giving, life-sustaining,
spirit-sourced, not yet stained with lunar rubescent flows,
they were taken, used, discarded and your sons—
tender hearts turned in ways you will never know,
were also taken, until finally you all fled.

You took to the heights, excavating deep into red-gold stone cliffs,
where you architectured a safe haven using clay and stone and there,
you remade yourselves, you recreated a brave new world
to live in, to love in, to hold onto and cherish.

No one could reach you in your Eagle's Nest—while you,
like the Eagles—Creator's own viceroys, loyal messengers all—
guarded your domain hidden under centuries of sheltering stone.

Relieved only by the bright winds on a summer morning
or on a winter's eve, forging toward you from each cardinal direction,
calling you to rest your sentinel eagle eyes, gazing all the daylong
and through the spangled nights at the desolate, dangerous, desert below.
Then, oh ancient ones, again, suddenly you were gone!
Did you lose sight of who you were? Of your spirit-selves?
Of your true point of origin? Did you forget your Creation stories?
Your ancestral lines drawn back to the Beginning and
your Spirit-given original instructions—sacred laws, sacred codes?
Did you disregard your clans; their teachings, gifts and powers?
Where were your chiefs, your ceremonialists, your spiritual leaders?
And did they approve of that extraordinary leave-taking?

Your minds must have broken into pieces as precious as
the remnants of your own lives—the thousand-fold pottery shards
you left behind—scattered helter-skelter in your abject desertion.

How could you have known then, that across the arc of time,
they would substantiate, in the most exquisite terms,
that you recognized the science of clay, water and fire;
that you realized the stunning aesthetics of functional beauty;
the alchemy of symmetry and style; and, in the profoundest sense,
that you understood through inspiration, vision and revelation, the
Spirit source of sacred art, sacred ways of being, sacred communion.

And so, on those fateful nights, your hearts sorrowful,
your spirits exhausted, you clambered down that ruddy cliff,
slipping and sliding under a blood-shot, fast retreating sky.

Rushing down to the unforgiving jagged canyon below,
descending from once-safe sheltered heights, you began
the long walk in abstracted, funereal silence, while across
the alloyed desolate expanse each attentive stone witnessed
the exodus of a whole people—heavy hearts entombed.

And as your hearts fell at your broken feet, did Earth reclaim
your salted blood?
Your sad, bewildered eyes and your sun-bleached bones
dying to the splendor of what once was?

Finally, at daybreak, and in the sounding radiance of Sun's
kept promise, did Creator gather up your wild and noble spirits,
like so many glimmerings of morning dew on cactus spines,
to show you the way home?

Legend

I was born from the blood and bones
of a murdered Sumerian God.

I was born from a rib of the first man born of clay
and the breath of a Punishing God.

I was born of a grain of golden sand and
the cosmic seed of a Creation-loving God.

I was born of an elm tree and
the beautiful dream of three Norse Gods.

I was born of an incestuous love between
Dawn Maiden and her rapacious Father God.

I was born of yellow corn, of golden eagle,
and the sun-drenched East wind.

I was born of silt made beautiful in a riverine swirl
and a Sky God's loving rainbowed glance.

I was born of Jaguar and Snake—someone was needed to tame Chaos.

I was born of Turquoise and Feather whose
exquisite loving was tended to by a Mountain God.

I was born when Coyote and Wild Cat kissed and the sky fell.

I was born in the South from yellow cornmeal and blue water,
kneaded by Earth Mother and baked to perfection by Father Sun.

I was born, bruised and Earth-bound, from the tears
of an all-seeing, blue-eyed Egyptian Sun God.

I was born under the African sky of Creator God and Sister Moon:
my river-blessed red clay body wrapped tight in night-silk—ink-blue.

I was born of stone.

Chieftain

In an Age of Stone,
a saturnine face was
chiseled grim by a Zephyr
color-washed sky blue,
as lovely and enduring
as she was precise in the incision.

Where had she learned his impassioned story
abiding still in the unmapped recesses of his great heart?
And why was his salt song still being sung?

This young Zephyr loved the mystery of him, returning
again and again on parched summer afternoons
to cool these sunbaked golden cliffs where all
living things in the surround welcomed
her blue-bright breezes—so lovely, so brisk.

While she, with searchingly incisive kinetic blade,
across aeonic strands of unwavering time,
engraved the calculus of his life:
inscribing her vigilant love in a monument
of stone, the color of the sun. Until one day,
in an ardent reveal, he appeared held rock steady
in the grip of a sun-bronzed cliff-face,
memorializing time like a lover's unfading memory.

And there's a primordial life-force about him,
rushing like Niagara falling, falling headlong.
But look! it's in his fathomless obsidian eagle eye,
that simply everything, *everything*, is said.

There is no, "Cease and desist!"
in any mineral atom of his stern profile. No.
Instead, his dark eyes proclaim a ferocity for life,
his penetrating gaze, like an arrow on target,
betrays highest merit, a nobility of intent,
and the message is as clear as dawning light—
the fiercest battle is yet to be won.

Refugee

"Mama, where are you?
Papa, why did you run?
Sister, where did those men take you?
Brother, you too?"

"What shall I do now?
Can I stay here?
Will those men return?"

Sister said, "Little one, run, now!"
Brother said, "Little jewel, hide now!"

"Mama, where are you?
Papa, will you come to find me?"

"I hear them now, someone is crying.
A sound of pain frightens me.
Is that Sister? No, that is Brother!
Who is crying that way?"

"Mama, where are you?
Papa, are you there?"

Sister cried, "Run!"
Brother whispered, "Hide!"
Where shall *I* run to?
Where *is* there to hide?

There is a hot wind,
there is a desert storm.
No one sees me.
I'm still as stone.
Now night has come.

Sister said, "Little one, run *now*!"
Brother said, "Little jewel, hide *now*!
"Mama, where are you?
Papa, they are coming … "

Selkie

Walking up to Castle Rock on a frosty, mist-veiled morning.
Rounding a bend on the mountain trail and there you are!
Selkie! You are a saltwater spirit of the magical kind!
Why are you beached on a mountaintop sister? Did you not have time
to *change*? To throw on your sealskin? To slip back into your
emerald sea-world, silent like the stars and deeper even still.

Who was it so beautifully captivated you my darling girl?
It must have been some handsome Celt who saw you shed your
glimmering moonstone seal-skin, and fell head over heels in love
with you dancing under a smiling moon, your small white feet
shining like pearls. And you saw him too and oh, you loved him!
It was too soon for you to tell that he was a man of the mountains.

At first, you made ready to run for the deeps, only it was too late.
You had gazed upon him while his heart made exquisite you, his.
And when he asked to take you to his mountain? "Yes!" You whispered.

Sweet child, how on earth were you to know about mountains?
How could you have known air and sky as dry as bone?
How were you to know the pain of keeping your lovely sea-wet body
dry and warm, in order to love a man, the way a woman does.

But with your gentle, unaffected Selkie soul, how could you not
but imagine only the good, the beautiful, the true?
You did not know a man's love could be this captivating—
the girth of love ever-tightening with each passing moon—
while your lunar-driven and salted green-blue love, ocean-deep
as it was, foundered in mountain shades; halted in its tidal embrace.

How were you to know, in the darkest of night, that your land-love
would cruelly hide away your seal-skin—your life-line home?
It almost killed you to unearth it as, with fingers all a-tremble,
you slipped secretly into the sea-green skin—to become again everything
you had always known yourself to be. But now, on the mountain top, stalled,
with nowhere to go, hoarfrost burning into your fragile sealskin,
there was no turning back—there was only turning into stone.

Citadel

Citadel: broken, abandoned, shouldering the weight of times past.
There remains no safe path leading to the safety of your fortress walls;
walls carved out of red stone, the color of dried blood.

But once, on this lonely land, stone-bound, you held your ground,
protected your noble crusading knights, confirming their invincibility.

And you, Christ's defenders! For the sake of a Holy Roman Empire
and the Pope in Rome, you wreaked your vengeful wars on a Holy Land
not yours by birthright, nor yours by lawful occupation, but by what
you were told was the wish of Jesus of Nazareth, a carpenter by trade
who revisioned the Word of his Jewish God, Yahweh, in a New Testament
you probably never read—not being literate by any measure.

Still, you left your homelands. You set out for the sun-bronzed expanses
of that carpenter's own Holy Ground. On prancing armored warhorses
you came shining metallic with embossed shields boasting your Coats of Arms
and swords in jeweled hilts; and flowing robes of finest linen bearing crosses
red as ruby, dark as blood running on a Day of Reckoning.

And what was that nefarious stated intention made in Rome amidst
fragrant clouds of sweet frankincense and myrrh, signed by Pope Urban II?
"Holy Lord of Hosts, grant us thy blessings and grace, that we may retrieve
all of your Holy Land and all treasures thus made ours by your victory
in Heaven as it is on earth. Holy Son of God, assist us with your mighty sword
to wreak vengeance on all who stand in our way! Upon our sacred troth,
we will leave no man, woman or child who know you not, alive."

I wonder what that young part-time laborer, part-time Rabbi, wandering
the holy hills of Judea, a thousand years ago and serving his community
as both prophet and rebel, would have said to this *spin*—a Holy War!

Citadel! Beyond your own virtuous disintegration, see there the
stone cadavers of all your brother fortress strongholds across the Holy Land.
Once formidable and to the very last, like you, they held fast until the end:
Krak de Chevalier, Montfort, Belvoir, Atlit, Arsuf, Acre and *Caesarea*
guarded every approach to Jerusalem: and yes, in the First Crusade,
Jerusalem was indeed taken by knights in shining armor but at what a blood-price!

To Pope Urban in Rome, Raymond of Aguilers victoriously reported:
"In the Temple of Solomon, Christian knights rode in blood up to their knees
and their steeds up to their bridle reins!" Fulcher of Chartres, with pride unbridled,
said this: "In the Temple Mount, in Jerusalem, 10,000 were killed … we were
up to our ankles in blood. None were left alive; neither women nor children."

Was the young carpenter, teaching a Jewish revisional message of love,
of forgiveness and peace—was he watching?

It was the time for you, great Citadel—victorious, impenetrable,
true as stone—to show your mettle: unassailable under siege.
On your unscalable mountain top you could proudly display
your defensive measures: your crenelated battlements crowned
with foreboding assault towers; your powerfully wrought
double-towered barbican, built to oversee the drawbridge and
to protect, Citadel, you and yours—at all cost. And then your
castle-keep, maintaining the ferocious interiority of your fortified self
with a stone heart beating as strong and steady as a homing device.

And then great bastion, not too long in coming, the Second Crusade.
Flourishing were Jerusalem, Edessa, Antioch and Tripoli with their mighty
fortresses—your compatriots all—unconquerable, no matter the approach.
But now, warriors from Arabia, from the deserts of Syria and Iraq;
the Seljuk Turks from the North and the Egyptians from the South
turned to the violent reclamation of their own patrimony, their own Holy Land.
And it was a mighty force! Do you remember Citadel?

And why are my eyes brimming with tears? Why does my own heart break?
Over time Zangi, Nur al din, Shirkuh, Saladin, Al-Malik al-Kamil, lion-hearts
on Arabian stallions—wielding moon-blessed scimitars, sliced through your
knightly forces like lightning on the run to the Gates of Paradise.
It was indeed a final reckoning; it might indeed be called by some,
a judgement from Heaven.

And so, with the first crusading victory obliterated, a plague of humiliation spread
across the Western World sounding a death knell that released the hounds of hell.
And with the tolling of that bell came a call across Christendom for restitution.
A vengeance *ad infinitum,* biblically endorsed, that allowed for no Saracen man,
woman or child to be left alive.

I really don't see an end to it, do you?
And so, towering Citadel, I stand here below you,
small under the silent shadow of your own dénouement.
I *hear* well-nigh eight centuries of siege and retribution
encrypted in your definitive silence—an unending defeat in aggregate.

I *see* your mortared shoulders and arms, your mineral strength,
your chivalrous heart weathering on this great clifftop.
A granite Goliath architectured in stone,
you have finally surrendered to the inexorable
surgical winds of the Siroccos.
Like a great hero of the old time, you have capitulated to
to every splicing needle of liberating rain
on every frozen starstruck desert night.

And here, because I now call you friend,
Citadel, I stand resolute with you in this catastrophic air.
I know the weight of the sentinel sorrow you carry on
remnant shoulders of iron.
I see it lodged in your ever-haunted eyes,
and I have read this anthology of stone held so close
to a vigilant heart worn down by time and time again.

Hecate

Mighty basilisk, magical, and mysterious, Hades' beloved
standing guard over his morose and shadowed world, yes!
But oh, my Goddess! When you appear on the surface of things!

Yet, when under a quiet new moon, stepping forth into
your reflective glimmerings of braided light:
silver and gold entwined raining down on an
acquiescent world, Lady, I see you differently—you shine.

I found you Hecate, where you are rightfully to be found—
at the gates of Hell—at every cruel or worse, disappointing juncture.
Not knowing where to turn, in need of a working curse and in lieu
of any coherent response from a more principled God,
it was you, dark Goddess who answered my call.

Yes, it was you who gravely listened, while we together
patiently, uncovered with deserved reverence, each secret wound,
each lacerated line of this daughter's once unblemished mind:
the stifled screams, the tears withheld, those forbidding silences—
ventricular, auricular abrasions securing a heart now turned to stone.

And it was you, strange Goddess, who celebrated my righteous rage
asking for nothing in return but to remember, with all due respect, *your* gift
and to place *you*, front and center, in thought, word and deed
when facing any of life's provocations that entailed fear or self-doubt
or represented certain blunt force trauma to the heart.

I was to love and revere you, as you would me beloved,
no matter the state of peril at hand, no matter how dark the darkest path
might be, leading into the light—a beloved paradox.

And so, across the particular space and time it takes to live any singular life,
Hecate, using her dark fire and my stone heart, has forged
this fragmented and flawed Self into a singular laser-like flame that,
like the steel of a Samurai sword, can slice a spring wind, raining
a thousand cherry blossoms down on a yielding ground of love.

Cretaceous

From one mother to another,
transcending species,
transcending time.

Where did you come from sister?
When did you once roam free?

Something petrified you enough
to turn you to stone …
and there, clinging ferociously,
with a relentless death-grip on life
and a fierce willingness to follow you
in every circumstance, at all cost,
is your sweet babe-in-arms.

Mother's true, know this,
as do you and I.

I *see* you stone sister …

Was it that your roseate baby, being so small,
fell prey to a cruel early calcification—
a misfortune of immense proportion?

And that you, with your unhesitating mother's heart,
wrapping your great wings around the tiny one,
nestling in his favorite spot, in the warm base of your neck,
you moved mineralized into this world, forever together?

I am here now with you, in this garden of the gods
where distinct beings, like you and I, meet in a given moment.
In this stone temple, I gaze upon you both in wonder—
mother and son merged in stone the color of the setting sun.

Beings as warm and infused with love and life as any other.

Aztec

Priest, you may have been the only *tlamacazui* left to rue
the loss of our Empire of the Sun. With a heart as heavy
as the ground itself, you vowed, as many of us did, to remain
in the only way possible—cast in stone—so that you could speak
in the ways of the Great Mystery to any one with a listening heart.

In those shining days Priest, we welcomed your telling
of our beloved *Aztlan*—and of our great Gods; of the
rainbow-feathered serpent, *Quetzalcoatl*; of the God of Rain, *Tlaloc*
and of our Hummingbird War God, *Huitzilopochtli*.

And oh, Priest, how your heart beat when you sang of
our Earth Mother, *Tonantzin*! She, who kneaded people from corn
and breathed her sacred breath into us in order that we may live,
love, pray and die into her own life-sustaining, green-gold body.

But now, here you are Priest, with me, in this forlorn world.
You have become an East-facing stone temple. And I,
I was born again with an ancient heart and blood as old,
running lines of deep memory through time-worn veins.

And I return again and again to sit beside you, here on this
weather-hewn altar stone. And I will listen when you speak
of that time, when on our holy lands, temple-shrines were placed
four-squared to honor the sacred directions. A time when, all,
when everyone breathed and lived and celebrated everything at
the center of our Azteca world, in *Tenochtitlan*.

And I will hear you tell of how our *tlatoani*, our high kings,
were mighty even then and how our *pipiltin*, our nobles,
were wise in all the ways of Heaven and Earth.

Priest! Do you remember our God-inspirited warrior clans?
Our *Ocēlōtl*, Jaguar warriors in capes of black and gold,
wielding long spears, obsidian-sharp and true.
And our Eagle warriors, *Cuāuhtli* with eagle feather
headdresses and capes shining black and white under an
Aztec sky—turquoise shot through with gold—colors of the Gods.
We could almost hear the hearts of the humble countryfolk
beat faster at the approach of our armies. We also saw how
those innocent ones: the strong for slavery, the virginal for sacrifice,
collapsed at the sight of our warriors appearing like lightning,
like waves of black thunder rolling—a seasonal tsunami of death.

And we watched in fierce silence as they fell to their deaths ...

Priest, as you had prophesied, we Aztecs indeed became
masters of our world. Oh! And how beautiful was that world!
How beautiful was our sacred *Tenochtitlan*!

May I tell some of our story too? We had everything
did we not? All the peoples of the world, fearful and reverent,
came to trade, to marvel! How could they not? With
our graceful lattice of clean-water canals throughout the golden city;
our sacred precincts hallowed by the Great Temple and other splendors,
like you, Priest, now set in stone before me! Yes, we had everything!
Tobacco, cacao, corn, cotton, beans, slaves, jade, gold and amber
sacrificial virgins, and gardens worthy of the Gods! The world was ours!

But then, Priest, do you remember the dark days?
What about when those *Tlaxcala* and *Huexotzingo*
warriors who defeated our once-invincible Jaguar and Eagle warriors?

You said you had spoken strong-heartedly with the Gods and
that we were not giving our all to them! You said they wanted more
and then even more than that. And we did as you said.

But then Priest? When *everything* had been given to *every* God!
Do you now remember Priest? Do you remember when
there was no more left to give? And when there was nothing left
and on that darkest of all days, you came to us and said,
"The Gods have spoken again ... ."

And, under the last jade and gold and cobalt Aztec sky
we would ever know, the color of all our blood sacrifices
sinking into the last setting sun, you, in your Jaguar robe
and all the people watched high king, *Cuauhtemoc* freely
offer our city, our lives and our world to the Conquistador.

Ganesh

Even you Elephant God, Ganesh, Lord of all Beings,
you with one thousand sacred names, even you need to sleep.

You were ill-conceived from the start all because of
a moment of treacherous love leading to a misguided reaction
of celestial proportion—Lord Shiva and Devi Parvati,
your divine parents, striving to best each other, in the name of love.

And so, out of their cosmic impertinence—you, killed
by your jealous father then brought back to life imperfectly
by your rightfully enraged mother—Creator Brahma took
and formed you anew. And in the re-making, in a fit of pure poetics,
he designed you as both man and elephant, announcing throughout
Creation that you were to be the most beloved of all Gods.

Lord Ganesh, this song is my mantra yoga—my own holy chant
celebrating your myriad Self—and so I meditate your
appearance before me in this natural stone—your sweet sleep.

I sing your sacred names, all the while reflecting the
illuminating wisdom traditions housed within each one.

You are a powerhouse deity indeed!
And I remember experiencing you as such
in an exquisitely life-threatening encounter.
As Lord of Prosperity, *Ganapati*, you might be
the most hardworking God in the Hindu pantheon!

And what are your empyrean gifts?
Well, you gave me exactly what I prayed for.
Exactly when I prayed for it!
But I had not a whit of an idea that there would be
a price to pay—pain, fear and sorrow, misguidance.
I am now careful in the extreme with what I ask of you.
Not that I'm afraid, on the contrary, I am reverent, respectful,
thoughtful, in a word, more cautiously precise.
You taught me how to pray.

But to come to you is no easy matter, for as *Amit*,
Incomparable Lord, you ask much of the human soul.
You teach that to draw near to you requires
purity of thought, heart, soul and body—
How on earth is that even possible for a mere human?
You are a hard task-master indeed!
After all, as humans, Lord Ganesh, are we not by definition,
are we not all by nature, walking-wounded? Still and all,
what must we do? Those of us who long to approach you?
To know you? To touch the jeweled hem of your sacred garment?

You say that we must come to know you, as *Avaneesh*,
Lord of the World; and as the celestial guardian of the
Muladhara Chakra: that wondrous sacred source
of our body-being, our spirit-being, our whole being!

Then you, as *Bhupati*, Lord of the Gods, ask us to stabilize
our own inner ground so that we may know and experience
ourselves in our original unimpaired state-of-being.

And as *Alampata,* Eternal Lord, you who loves Earth our mother
and all beings who live upon and within her;
it is you who teaches that if we desert her, we abandon also
Creator's infinite and eternal dream of Creation.
And how, as *Buddhinath,* God of Wisdom, would you respond
to our abandonment of Earth over whom you watch
as fiercely as you would your very own daughter?

Lord Ganesh says: "To receive divine knowledge and Heaven's grace,
you must first love yourselves deeply into this world. Yes, with all its
imperfections, impossible paradoxes, with all its incandescent beauties."

Then as *Bhalchandra*, you, Moon-Crested Lord,
who oversees Creation from the invisible to manifest wonder,
you demand that we honor all of life for its sublime beauty,
essential integrity and ultimate relevance. Only then,
will you bring yourself as *Buddhividhata*, God of Knowledge
to the seeking soul. Only then, can we learn from you how to
successfully negotiate the obstacle course that defines
and charts for each of us, our own destined lives.
Lord Ganesh, beyond your myriad named depictions, I also see
the holy items you carry with you—your own teaching tools.

Your broken tusk—

        we are all damaged goods.

Your noose—

        no one avoids paying necessary consequences.

Your sacred rosary beads—

        constant prayer is as necessary to life
        as oxygen is to carbon dioxide,
        as the moon is to the ocean tides.

Your sacred spear—

        some things warrant defending
        or fighting to the death for.

A bowl of candy—

        we cannot carry on the journey without respite,
        without heavenly fragrances, love,
        and other sweeter things.

Macaw

Sacred bird, do you remember
your cardinal birthplace in the South?
Where the steaming jungle undergrowth,
moist with cloud and warm rains cushions
Earth's rising to meet the dawning light?
Where your own kith and kin—feathered jewels
choreographing arcs of flashing light—fell
like a thousand fragrant blossoms through the
rainforest, itself an almost impossibly prismatic green;
a green like lemon and lime, conjugated.

Someone said you were sanctified. As a messenger for
ancestors and gods, how could you not be?
But that was a harsh Mandate of Heaven was it not?

For eons you were hunted, caged, and traded
by your captors with people from the far North
for precious turquoise and silver. And there, the people
sacrificed your own precious life to enhance themselves
in your own prismatic splendor; weaving, hemming, interlacing
their ceremonial regalia with your rainbow feathers,
iridescent, and all a-shimmer, sacred like rain,
sacred like stars in the heavenly skies.

A treasured gift from distant gods: you were and still
are my relative, legendary. After all, how could anyone
calculate the true value of Sun's light held radiant in
your multihued wingspread? And you, you were
held captive to the dazzling myth *they* wove around you.

Born anciently, even now, you are a mythic guardian of the South.
It's an inner orientation, a directional dwelling place of the soul
where Life-Giver shines in the brightest of skies; where earth and air,
rain and winds are tranquil; where love is free and strong;
where light and dark play in the deep end and where souls,
finally released, begin their journey to the other side of
the star-deep trail that crosses the midnight sky.

Beautiful bird, you were bewitched,
as they danced and prayed and sang to you.
Bewildered and bemused, how could you not,
reveal your own soul's secret? Your god-gifted sacred wisdom—
how to run that curving Rainbow Bridge straight from Earth
into the waiting arms of Heaven in lived and knowing ways.

Macaw says, "Being rainbow comes first." This is her song ...

I am Red, mercurially in flux, my metaphysics is
constant becoming—I am a dance.

I am Orange, beloved child of red and gold aureate,
strong, enduring, I am a creative, I am one
who stands my ground.

I am Yellow, father Sun's divine prerogative.
I am the light of love, and with that love-light, life affirming and brave.

I am Green, I am Earth-in-her-body being.
I am a renewal: the color of life—its beginning, its end.

I am Turquoise, veined contrary across a shock
of blue as vast as a dancing New Mexico sky.

I am Indigo, deep as an unsolved mystery,
containing all night skies, all dark radiance.

I am Violet, an intermingled love-child of
red and blue who dance through any given life like
oxygen in the artery, like blood in the vein.

Sacred bird, Keeper of the Rainbow
forgive us, for we know not what we do ...

She-bear

My bear sister is made up of Sun's light.
We've been together since the beginning—
eternally recurrent in each other's lives.
In this life she presents as a Kodiak—in fact, she is an ethereal.

I recall exactly the first moment we met in *this* life.
It was a rescue of the first order—we tend to reunite that way!
We are found to each other in the enchanted regions of the soul
where things in their *true nature* breathe and live.
In one moment, she is my teacher and I her disciple,
and the next, I, her mistress and she my attendant;
then again, we are boon companions, confidantes,
and travelers of the best kind—unafraid of the unknown.

Here and now, in early morning misted mountain glens,
beside murmuring sky-watered rivers or forested valleys,
we take our rest on a sun-tended stone slab and deep-talk,
as sisters often do, of strength, of vulnerability, of how to endure.

And on this spring day, with you, my bear-sister, beside me,
warmed by soft shafts of even warmer sunlight, we sit
silent, in perfect repose *because* we are here, together.
We know Time is taking his time with us.
The morning breeze listens in as trees sigh, stones sing,
and mountains echo in the surround, while Earth
rises splendid under a perfectly unmatched blue sky.

And you bear-sister, broad in the shoulder, golden haired,
you have sculpted your life to secure what you know
to be your own true nature, as I too have endeavored to secure
a favorable fit in this body-being, in this world, in the spite of the
endless incongruities—the impossible paradox.

Here, with each other, we speak the in the way stones do:
we have listened to an infinitude of silence;
we have tasted stone as has our blood and tears.
To stone, salt is the essence of Heaven, the flavor of God.
And, like stone, you my bear-sister and I have tasted forever.

Sheer

What joy!

This caramel and burnt topaz multiplication of matter
caught fast in a cyclonic reach for an endless sky and God.

This disordered geometry of lithic longing:
a petrified rush of fire in the blood reaching for
the urgent union of a perfect kind of other love.

When this stone was in its original being—
a river of fire created in the image of its Maker,
his first love song was a genesis of all possibility …

But, as too often happens with all bright beginnings,
with its first reality-sting came a broken-hearted lament
sung with such sweet sorrow, sweet as stolen honey, that
even stars fell pell-mell out of a blue-stone, hurdy-gurdy sky.

He was after all, only a fire-river touched newly by a cooler kind
of Earth-bound love whose relentless oncoming caresses
captivated, catalyzed and finally fully encrusted his once molten,
freely blazing heart in her mantle, shimmering in bronze and gold.

Ceremony

Four gracious stones stand in abstracted silence—
an architectured rhapsody of sandstone—chaos
reaching for dawn's splendid inauguration:
a new day designed to be new, to be sacred,
to be significant—replete with second chances.

Yes, even stones, rise to the waking day, turning
toward, welcoming, a great-hearted Sun.

In their graceful up reach, even stones know,
with their insistent song, how to offer holy
offerings of love, respect and appreciation
—gratitude for the gift of another day.

And you, you who so easily disregard dawn,
not knowing the difference between the day,
as it is and the day to be lived as *yours*.

You, who so unthinkingly walk ahead into your days,
with no consideration of the deeper mysteries involved,
the greater joys, the higher purpose, the shadow's need
and the pitfalls ahead; you become so easily handled,
blinded to the chains that bind you to the elemental day,
and the constant inadequacies of its fruitless remains …

And do you not understand that *that* unlived day's heart broke?
And that, yes, all the days yet to be lived, still unowned, will also
fall from Grace, crushed under your persistently oblivious feet?

Solitude

There is no mystery

        in the destined gaze

                of a brooding stone.

Aperture

This empty sky
seems to me
a lingering lament—
time spent in time
dissolved into monolithic days,
gazing at the silver edge of things and
waiting for the formality of that moment
in the particular—
the final leave-taking …

Archetype

A stone is, of course,
always a stone
but is also not.

Do you *see* this one?
Through the phenomenon?
It's transparencies fully revealed?

And who is it then, appearing before you?
Do you see what I see?
This stone as *being*—in and of and beyond itself?
Emerging force-filled, ferocious, like a
Gilgamesh, an Achilles, an Arjuna, a Beowulf—
telling of ancient heraldic worlds,
indestructible, fully apparent in the
divine order of things,
with their incandescent beauties and
untroubled subjection to seasonal change.

In other words—
stone fully surrendered to the notion
of one day, finding itself in a
a small perfectly replicated pebble,
in some small child's glad hand,
then whisked away to sit amongst
her treasured collection,
placed carefully, precisely so,
on a very happy windowsill.

The Fall

Stones fallen from grace, each named and wounded,
tumbled and crushed in a composite embrace
caustic as the snow-white burn of salt in the cicatrice.

I sit here by their side in this abstracted stony silence
falling all around, hard like iron, under an ashen sky,
and I recall that great gods and even greater goddesses often
make their appearance as a lovely greening mist; in this case,
bittersweet, like the ironic innocence of a newly dawning day.

This is no casual solitude. The mythic weight of stone in this
wooded winter glen is as heavy as a vanquished warrior
and his boon companions laying down weary hearts
on battle-bruised ground. And I feel the need, somehow,
to make amends—to put up a Sending Spirits On ceremony.

I'll imagine this day burning fiercely with archetypal sacrifices.
I'll place an angel of mercy, in white alabaster, to stand guard in the North;
in the South, a blue-green serpentine shield will hang from a silver-lit tree
while an obsidian-tipped arrow slung on an anciently-carved cedar bow
will rest against a fallen stone in the West, and a red jade chalice
will ornament the East where all tears, all incomplete thoughts,
all unrealized dreams are safely housed.

And, at the center of this disordered rockfall
a sacred fire, proportionate to the immensity of the moment,
will blaze fragrant with sweet cedar, bay laurel and juniper,
and I'll offer libations—pure spring water; honeyed milk;
food offerings—grains and healing herbs;
spirit gifts—prayers and strong-hearted songs.

When it is finished, walking away from this silent injured terrain—
a congress of stones entombed, each in its own beautiful enigma—
I reach out to the warmth of the everyday-world knowing
the miracle of Time's kindly dispersion of all sorrows
in the bright light of a new day.

Truth

It seems to me a truth is
only in the given moment true ...

Everything else, simply put,
is merely a subdivision of vocabularies
scored by sinuously ideational tracks:
thought-roads, side-walked
by antinomies a mile-wide,
leaving us to wonder if indeed—
in terms of consciousness—
it may be the side-walking thoughts,
unruly because unbound,
that form the truer *via regia*—
that "royal road" to the soul along which
we walk, constantly searching, inquiring,
skirting the edge, constantly losing our bearings,
constantly reaching for the beyond of things ...

While the ordinary people's road—*via vulgaris*
is laid down precisely to ensure for structurally
conditioned and capitulated thought-forms,
directionally mapped to stay on a well-tracked,
well-signed course of stasis in the guise of action,
and where all safely designed on and off thought-ramps
take you exactly to where you have been convinced
you need to be and where you need to stay put
safe and sound ...

Wall

Is there anything more beautifully integral,
more trustworthy than a wall of pure stone?

Possibly ...

But you! You, rock-solid kernel of iron truth,
you are a meteoric child of Sky and Earth.
Like a unified presence of angels quivering
between stone on stone, you are a blazing immensity,
that has me stopped dead in my tracks!

Do I run or stand my ground?

I should breathe ...

The monumental geology of your perfect stillness
belies the fact of you over millennia, withstanding
the onslaught of gale-force winds, storms of ice and rain,
and all the while, holding resolute, staying true to the line,
while Sun, your father, in his emphatic blue sky
uses your heroic granite girth as a daily practice range
for his javelin beams of light to find their mark.

Then again, look! Nourished by the rain-washed air, this crevice
folded in between the above and below of you is oxidized
burnt orange, weaving beautifully into calcinated streams of
sea-green flowing between the vibrating stone sheer that is you.

And when you send out your evening salt song, stars awaken,
then moon drops her light on your shoulders and you fall asleep
under the night sky, until dawn appears in a mother-of-pearl
early morning sky, and soon the blazing, day-bringing light
of your own beloved star and mine smiles on a waking world.

It is just that simple …
and this is me enchanted, and dreaming
that this wall of stone is dreaming of me.

Shiprock

You are an implacable solitude
interwoven with an analectic of stone.
Stationed at the borderland of where-ever
in this empyrean cobalt silence,
I hear your long-submerged heart begin to beat—
and a soul seed is germinating carefully, within
this lovely disintegrating body of red-gold stone.

Friend of my own heart, there you stand, caught up
in the immense experience of being stone
as I too, am spirit-caught in experiencing myself as human,
and in this sense, we are both immensities diminished
by space and time to take a stand on *this* particular ground of being.

I see the star-lines of your spirit as you must see mine:
the inner secrets of the soil that foundation the interior geography
of our souls. As for me, too many inner secrets are soiled—
sea-rivered with the blue and the red: briny courses rushing
through the arterial and venal byways of my own lived life—
keeping me staked to my own claim.

As for you, my Shiprock friend, I think
I know the weight of sorrow falling hard
on your monolithic shoulders like iron-rusted rose.

And with you I celebrate the purity of this blue light
falling all around us—there's so little left till the final abrasion;
your disintegration into iron-red sand until the final form of you
appears—bedrock, pure and simple, in collectible fragments.

I feel for you and I, as this rapturous light falls
indiscriminately, like the gold in unrefined honey
combed on the wild side. Even this late afternoon breeze
is filled with a microcosmic storm of stone, and therein,
lies the fractured beauty of you and I.

Stoned Love

There's a fire in the stone:
a convolution dissolving two souls
and releasing as fire does,
a hidden seed of love yearning to be set ablaze.

In their natural state—aeonic memory petrified—
stones are illuminated, transcendent beings:
supernatural: no more, no less.

They burn in the heat of a noon day sun,
dwell silently under bright surging seas
or fearlessly gaze from gleaming granite peaks
at distances and immensities impossible to fathom.

In the burning heart of stone
lies the history of all the world's loves
on replay—an infinity of recollection …

And I, a human solitary, wandering into
the tender silences of this limestone outcrop,
have come upon a chain reaction of geologic love—
two meticulously architectured mineral hearts
fused in a stone kiss, synchronized to perfection
within this vibrant air, deep and blue as Persian turquoise.

One stone embracing another,
as if, for the very last time—
a stunning intimacy.

Portrait

Something bored its way into
this tormented structure of stone
so deep as to tear the salt skin.

It's a brazen, enduring hit, like life itself ...

You withstood the cyclonic winds
hurtling down from the frozen North
sent by an inconsiderate, negligent god,
drilling down like a battering ram
to storm the walls of your great stone heart.

It's impossible to shake the vision of beauty in ruins ...

And you built that heart with courage unstoppable.
You stood your ground on a strength of purpose
as strong as the Sierra Nevada is rock solid.

You were indomitable in your aim
to endure your affliction.

You are beautiful, still!

Grinding Stone

Time out of mind, amidst the lithic remains of an ancient day,
when the center of the Old World described a woman's world,
and a hand-ground indented soft stone innovatively sculpted
became the heart of everything that sustained life.

Each lovely morning, when dawn rose to bring daylight
to a dreaming world, laughing mothers with children
and babes-in-arms came to this village of stone,
taking their rightful places, preparing for a good day.

Grandmothers, medicine women, and dreamers arrived
carrying river-reed baskets brimming with herbs and roots
while craftswomen, needleworkers, and hide tanners brought
feathers, bags of variegated clay, dyes and shell, and seed beads.

Gathered around their designated grinding stones
the village women sit and work, each to her own:
winnowing, cleaning, crushing and grinding her materials:
corn, acorns, barley, herbs and roots for nourishment
and strength, for prayer and healing, and for the sake of
beauty—food for the soul.

And craftswomen gathered to work with bone needles
while women, wise in the arts, prepared dyes:
black walnut, acorns, elderberries, and dogwood bark
to stain or paint sacred signs and symbols on skin, bone,
wood and clay—the earliest language systems we know.

But any human heart, pliable and expanding like a cloud
blossoming in the mercurial air, knows that without soul-tending,
functional necessity will not suffice to hold a people together;
knows that survival is always about community in the round.

And so, first a Blessing Prayer then a Spirit Calling Song,
then songs for all the days and ways of work and play and storytelling.
Stories to carry on a deeper knowing, to celebrate a greater kind of loving,
and the transporting of the whole heart of a brave and modest people.

Runes

Brooding, I gaze at this bronzed wall of weathered solid sand,
thinking of those stars constellated in the heavens, destined
to become the storytellers of our own human affections;
and thinking too, that stones—star people—like us, have lives to live;
have souls and yes, like us, they also dream.

I see my life storied on this timeworn cliff face etched by a
geometry of ancient runic lines, by which I read into
the metaphysics of my own lived life.

Age-old and time-honored, runic lore has me delving
into the mystery of living, loving relationship
between divinities and humans. And so, I read into
these elegantly lined forms running the expanse of this
precipitously embossed stone sheer—it's an instructional manual
written in the language of stone addressing the *now* in my life
and pointing me in new directions:

Nauthiz is the need-fire I must generate from within:
for the moment at hand is a fated one and consequences
must not fall fatal, as in times past. Need-fire will call in
Hagalaz, the hail-storm needed to bruise into life
a new possibility, just enough to augur in a new becoming;
a gentle germination under the care of *Ingwaz,*
in shaded places, in solitude, still and silent,
until new life awakens, emerging into the waiting arms of *Dagaz*—
dawn, waking from her starry sleep to a new day-dreaming world.

Daylight is indeed the great leveler. After all, no matter
what is said or left unsaid, no matter what is done or left undone,
no matter what is or may remain hidden, there is no escaping the light,
there is only denial, defiance and pretense.

Runestone, gazing at you, gazing at me—have you read me as deeply?
The bittersweet fragrance of my kind of silence? The lucent color and feel of me?
The multifaceted geology of my own complexed soul?

And, may I leave my own mark upon you?

Stone Silence

This solitary pilgrim by definition
understands that the infinite silence in stone
is the distilled word of a greater God—
the one that must needs remain unnamed.

Yet, *here* it is! In the fullness of perfection, of joy,
and to be freely plundered by this small wandering soul.

Stone was and is the first son and the first daughter of God.

It all comes down to stone—

Down to the stone silence
before the First Word was spoken.

Stone City

Here I am alone and in love with abandoned places,
where solitude is golden and the magic plain and simple,
there's really no place I'd rather be.

Imagined ancient metropolis, great hearted and abandoned,
I'm standing in the stone-cold shadow of your afflicted dream,
astounded at the sight of you, astonished at my own heart—
now beating sacramental—as I gaze upon your harrowed landscape:
a raveling out of ruined stones across a light-edged, razorbacked ridge,
glancing off a stone spur, sides sheered, jutting crags,
under a flood of stunning rose-gold and fast-ebbing sunlight
disappearing into a far-reaching vaulted sky, vivid with your
unwavering intent, celebrating the regal splendor of this culminating day.

Now, coming into closer contact with your storied ground:
the listening air drifting like a forgotten fragrance,
curls in and around your immense articulation of sheltering stones,
releasing a fragrant sanctity, an intoxicating palpitation:
an eternal flux in the still-current of life—the beloved paradox.

In the bright air, I hear your sad complaint in words and ways
riven in this late midsummer shimmer of heat, and now
I understand my place as witness to your extended demise.
I see your beautiful relic-being in my imagination,
I see the artifact of who you once were: a city of great moment,
of luminous spaces under the aquamarine wing of heaven:
ethereal, holy, magical, unrecoverable.

Battered by time and still defiant in your brazen stone beauty,
now, separation and loss are the condition of your remnant reveries
and you, you are still shouldering the crushing weight of your loss.

And yet, you radiate a vivid consciousness, an inner knowing,
as if you are still experiencing the very meaning of things.
For me, it is the mystical contact with your spirit of place, that
makes this a healing process where the divine and the mundane
converge into a pure interpenetration of human form and stone spirit:
nuanced, shaded, mysteriously harmonic, inseparable.
Stone city, when was it that you became dispossessed?
Who did you open your formidable gates to?
Was there a change in the air? Were there foretelling signs?
Here and now, I stand among the whispering remains
of your fallen world—as the same dangers approach my world.

You see, my world too is vulnerable at all times
to the whims of human nature, inhabited from the beginning
by the iron drive to war, even in peace, waiting, waiting
for the time to rage like a seasonal wildfire on the run—
some think of it as a sacrificial offering, a sacramental new beginning—
but as any good wildfire worth its salt and ashes knows,
the iron drive to war can mean nothing but destruction,
no matter the gunmetal rhetoric: protecting and defending
with the intent to make way for new opportunities, and in your time
ancient friend, your priests probably assured your good citizens that

taking up the sword was God's own invitation to a new life,
to new beginnings, in fact, a divine mercy in the making!

This fragile human culture—heart, mind and soul conjoined—
is the prime mover of our present, as it was for our past,
and will be in a future destined to be haunted by all
that has ever happened, by all that there ever was.

And so, here I stand, attentive to the enchantment of
this rain of light falling all around. Your pure woven limestone
now run through with gold, rippling along the crest
of your stony cliffs like a mountain lion on the chase.

And in this bronzed fading light, stone city, you are a testament
to the human soul's relentless architectural reach for heaven.
Indeed, even still you are a structured beauty dressed out
in red and gold, rising like a phoenix from scorched ground.
Once a magnificent edifice, now a ruin of your former self,
in the midst of this particular haunting, and because we humans
are by nature aesthetic creatures, I am obligated to sing this experience!

And you, who have shared your collective self simply by being
with me under this vacant sky reluctant to yield the day,
will you, in turn, my granite friend, sing your own canticle for me?
I am, you see, enchanted by the essence of you.
I hear your salt song in the whispering wind,
a limestone rhythm and rhyme.

I see your inner light, transcendent, holy, radiating
from within, and I am enveloped and drawn
into the ruined remains of your own legendary day.

Stone city, standing here on your own ground of being,
in your hallowed presence, I will sing you a stone song:

In the beginning, I too was stone.
I will be stone once again—and will join you,
forever, starstruck.

Milton Keynes UK
Ingram Content Group UK Ltd.
UKHW020614251123
433184UK00009B/165

9 781977 261151